Laramie

team mates

kArl MaLonE
and
ioHn StocKtoN

Robert Schnakenberg

THE MILLBROOK PRESS
BROOKFIELD, CONNECTICUT

Published by The Millbrook Press, Inc.
2 Old New Milford Road
Brookfield, Connecticut 06804

Photographs courtesy of Barry Gossage/NBA Photos: pp. 6, 44; Andy Hayt/NBA
Photos: pp. 17, 51, 64; Fernando Medina/NBA Photos: p. 26; Norm Perdue/NBA
Photos: pp. 32, 80; Sam Forencich/NBA Photos: p. 36; AP/Wide World Photos:
pp. 59, 82; Jeff Reinking/NBA Photos: p. 75 (left); Scott Breen/NBA Photos: p. 75
(right); Noren Trotman/NBA Photos: p. 88.

Library of Congress Cataloging-in-Publication Data
Schnakenberg, Robert
Teammates : Karl Malone & John Stockton / Robert Schnakenberg.
p.   cm.
Includes index.
Summary: A dual biography that emphasizes how greatly two Utah Jazz stars
rely on each other on and off the court and the extent to which their careers have
intertwined.
ISBN 0-7613-0300-6 (lib. bdg.)
1. Malone, Karl—Juvenile literature. 2. Stockton, John 1962– —Juvenile litera-
ture. 3. Basketball players—United States—Biography—Juvenile literature. 4.
Utah Jazz (Basketball team)—Juvenile literature. [1. Malone, Karl. 2. Stockton,
John, 1962– . 3. Basketball players. 4. Utah Jazz (Basketball team) 5. Afro-
Americans—Biography.] I. Title.
GV884.AlS35   1998
796.323'092'273—dc21
[B]   97-19765 CIP AC

conTeNts

fiRe anD ICe

What good would the

All-Star Game be without Magic and Larry? That's what a lot of people were wondering before the 1989 National Basketball Association All-Star Game in Houston. One of the largest crowds in NBA history had turned out for the event, only to learn that Magic Johnson, the best guard in basketball, and Larry Bird, the league's best forward, would both be sitting out because of injuries. Who would step up to take their places?

That day, the NBA introduced two rising stars to fans across the country. Karl

Malone, the muscular forward of the Utah Jazz, dominated the game with 28 points and 9 rebounds. He dunked, slashed, and powered his way to the hoop almost every time his team had the ball. And he did almost all of it on the receiving end of passes from his Utah teammate, point guard John Stockton. Playing in his first All-Star Game, Stockton assisted on 17 baskets and came in a close second in the voting for Most Valuable Player.

"I'd like to split this trophy right down the middle with that little guy," Malone said as he accepted the MVP award. He smiled as he pointed to his teammate, John Stockton.

"It seems like we have a connection with each other," Malone went on to say. "When he throws me the ball, it's his way of saying thanks for running the floor. When he gives you the ball, you can't really do anything but dunk it."

"That's Karl," said Stockton, his quiet, camera-shy partner. "Always taking care of his buddy Stock."

In the years since that All-Star Game, basketball fans everywhere have come to appreciate the special connection these two players share. As each has continued to grow and improve at his position, the other has benefited. Both hold a number of basketball records that could not have been achieved without the other. And when it came time to choose players for the "Dream Teams" that would represent the United States at the 1992 and 1996 Olympic Games, no one dreamed of including one without the other.

Most important, John and Karl have remained friends off the court as well. They talk on the phone, go out together, and support each other in interviews and with members of the press. To some people, this is amazing, given their very different backgrounds. John is white, a Catholic from Washington State, best known for his "technical" playing style. Karl is an African-American Baptist from northern Louisiana, best known for his physical style of play. How could two players as different as these possibly have the strong connection they do, both on and off the court?

To John and Karl, however, the answer was simple. Out on the hardwood they discovered how their differences could complement each other, making them both stronger. With John, at 6 feet 1 (185 centimeters) and slight of build, firing bullet passes, and Karl, 6 feet 9 (206 centimeters) and 250 pounds (113 kilograms), muscling his way to the hoop to score, the Utah Jazz became one of the NBA's best teams. Stockton and Malone made repeat trips to the playoffs, as well as to the NBA All-Star Game.

Always, they remained united by their love of basketball. That similarity was stronger than all their differences.

"We are going to be bonded at the shoulders for the rest of our lives," Karl has said of his relationship with John. "If we go to the Hall of Fame, they probably want us to be there at the same time. There's no person I'd rather be connected with than John."

Their fans around the country agree. To most people, it's become impossible to think of one without the other. As Sam Smith, a sportswriter in Chicago, wrote after another outstanding All-Star performance by the Utah twosome, Stockton and Malone are "like a couple of guys playing a kids' game exceptionally well: black and white, fire and ice. They're different, but they fit together perfectly."

The story of how they came together begins in two very different places: Spokane, Washington, and Summerfield, Louisiana. Both towns remember them by the sound of a dribbled basketball. . . .

2

dReaMing oF the NBA

Long into the night, the sound of a bouncing basketball could be heard up and down North Superior Street in Spokane, Washington. It was John Stockton again. No matter what the weather, he would be out there shooting at the hoop suspended at the end of his family's long sloping driveway. Sometimes he liked to pretend he was Gus Williams, the star guard of the Seattle SuperSonics. John was small, but he always dreamed that one day he, like Williams, would be a great player in the NBA.

That ritual went on for years. "I remember driving by Stockton's house in high school," said one of his neighbors, Mark Rypien. "Ten, eleven o'clock at night, and he was out on the driveway dribbling a basketball." Mark Rypien would go on to become a sports champion too, as the starting quarterback of the Washington Redskins. Another star athlete, the baseball player Ryne Sandberg, also came from that area.

John Houston Stockton was born on March 26, 1962. His father, Jack Stockton, was the co-owner of Jack & Dan's Tavern, a bar where many of the people of Spokane gathered. John's mother, Clementine—called "Clemmy"—stayed at home and raised the family. John had an older brother and two sisters.

The Stocktons were a close-knit Irish family, who fit in well with Spokane's large Irish Catholic population. In fact, John's neighborhood was known as the "Little Vatican" because so many of the boys who lived there grew up to become priests. Bing Crosby, the singer and actor who played priests in many of his films, also grew up in Spokane. Although John went to church regularly, he chose not to follow in the footsteps of these others. His real passion, from an early age, was basketball.

When he wasn't out practicing by himself, John played one-on-one with his brother, Steve. Because Steve was four years older, and much taller, he usually got the better of John. "Those were rough games and I'd get knocked around," John later admitted. But the desire to beat his brother only made him more determined to improve his play. And it was the challenge posed by the older, bigger, and stronger boys in the neighborhood that inspired him to find a way to do it.

Always small compared with the other boys in the neighborhood, John got tired of getting pushed around on the basketball court. One day, when John was about 12 years old, he came home crying to his father. It had been an especially bad day on the playground. John was on the verge of quitting. His basketball career could have ended right there. "Maybe you shouldn't play with those boys," Jack Stockton counseled him. "Maybe they're too rough." John didn't like the suggestion that he was too small to play his favorite game. Instead of quitting, he returned to the playground. "I went back out to show them I could play," he said.

bLAziNG sPeeD Basketball is thought of as a big person's game. However, many of its greatest stars, like Bob Cousy and Isiah Thomas, have been short. Even very small players, like Muggsy Bogues and Spud Webb, became successful by learning how to pass, steal the ball, and run around taller opponents. This was the kind of game John Stockton decided to develop. He worked hard on his ball-handling skills, and joined the school track team to improve his quickness and stamina. Now, when he went out to play against taller boys, he blew around them with blazing speed and scored easy baskets. His teammates came to appreciate his skill at distributing the basketball, because for them it meant more chances to score. Suddenly, the small, wiry boy who couldn't shoot over people became very popular. John had learned, as one of his NBA coaches later put it, "that if you pass the ball you always get a ride home."

John attended elementary school at St. Aloysius, a Catholic parochial school five blocks from his house. After school he would practice basketball, then meet his father at Jack & Dan's Tavern. Sometimes he would ask his dad for a quarter to buy french fries at the restaurant across the street. Oftentimes Jack Stockton would ride home on John's bicycle, with John perched up on the handlebars, enjoying the ride. Jack and Clementine Stockton liked basketball almost as much as John did. Their favorite player was Bob Cousy. But they never dreamed that their son would go on to be as great as the legendary "Cooz." "The only person in the world who thought John would play in the NBA was John," Jack Stockton later said.

In high school, at Gonzaga Prep, John began changing people's minds about that. Gonzaga ("The second syllable is like the 'zag' in 'zigzag'" John likes to point out) was another Catholic school, only a mile's drive from John's house. John entered at only 5 feet 5 (165 centimeters) tall and 90 pounds (40 kilograms), but with unusually large feet and hands for his size—perfect for gripping the basketball. Once again, John was in the shadow of his brother, Steve. As a Gonzaga baseball pitcher, Steve had once struck out Ryne Sandberg three times in one game. John rose to the challenge with some athletic exploits of his own. As a point guard on the Gonzaga Prep basketball squad, he enjoyed a 42-point game against star player Mark Rypien of rival Shadle Park High School. And while it was Rypien who went on to win a state championship and be named tournament MVP in his senior season, it was John Stockton who began to draw the attention of recruiters as a potential collegiate star.

One recruiter who didn't try to get John to come to his school was George Raveling, the coach at Washington State. Raveling thought John looked too young to be a big-time basketball player. Even though John had grown to 6 feet (183 centimeters), he still feared the point guard was too small to succeed. Dan Fitzgerald of Gonzaga University knew better, however, and he signed John to play at his school, just four blocks away from the Stockton home. "George Raveling didn't come after John and later admitted it was the biggest mistake he ever made," said Fitzgerald. Sometimes the people from your own neighborhood know you best.

Until he got to college, it seemed that the closest John Stockton would ever get to the NBA was his one evening as a ball boy at a Seattle SuperSonics exhibition game at the Spokane Coliseum. Now, as he enrolled at Gonzaga University, he would have a real chance to work toward his dream. He set out to make the most of it.

John knew Gonzaga University well. After all, it was the same college his father had attended. What was more, he had been sneaking into the Gonzaga gym to shoot baskets and play pickup games all through high school. "I never consciously thought about going all the way through the 'Gonzaga farm system,'" John later said, "but that's the way it happened."

As a freshman in 1980–1981, John didn't get much of a chance to earn a place in Gonzaga history. He played sparingly and averaged only 3.1 points per game. Even more disappointing was John's assist total, an average of barely one assist per game in his freshman season—not sufficient for a point guard hoping to impress his coaches with his passing skills. The following year, however, he upped that average to five assists a game. He contributed 11.2 points per contest as well. John was beginning to develop the all-around game he felt sure would take him to the pros.

In his junior year, John continued to improve. He posted marks of 13.9 points and 6.8 assists a game. Finally, in his senior season of 1983–1984, John had a true "break-out" campaign. He improved again in both major offensive categories, leading the West Coast Athletic Conference in scoring with a 20.9 average, as well as in assists and steals. He was chosen conference Most Valuable Player, and was selected as a second team All-American. For his 107-game career at Gonzaga, John had averaged 12.5 points and 5.2 assists while making 56 percent of his shots. These were statistics any NBA point guard would be proud of. Now he faced the prospect of the NBA draft. John had to hope that the pro scouts would overlook his size and small-school background and give him the chance to repeat that production in the big leagues.

One early indicator that John Stockton *would* be drafted came during the trials for the 1984 Olympic basketball team. Coach Bobby Knight had to select two point guards to bring with him to the Games in Los Angeles. Although John played better than anyone else in the trials, in the end Knight chose his own player, Indiana's Steve Alford, but John had proved to everyone that he was among the three top collegiate point guards in the nation. Now the only question was, what team would take a chance on him?

On draft day in 1984, John waited nervously while some of the best young players in America were chosen in the first round: Michael Jordan,

AT GONZAGA UNIVERSITY, JOHN DEVELOPED THE BALL-HANDLING SKILLS THAT HE WOULD LATER DEMONSTRATE IN THE PROS, AS HE DOES HERE IN A GAME AGAINST THE L.A. CLIPPERS.

Charles Barkley, Hakeem Olajuwon. Many of them would go on to become the NBA's all-stars. It seemed like an endless well of talent. That's why a lot of people were surprised when the Utah Jazz picked John. After all, the Jazz already had a good point guard, the All-Star Rickey Green, and nobody knew if the relatively unknown 6-foot-1 player from Gonzaga would be able to make it in the tough, physical pro game. Shortly after he was selected, John took a phone call from the Jazz television broadcaster, "Hot Rod" Hundley.

"Is everyone booing?" John asked sheepishly.

"No, they're not saying 'Boo,'" said Hundley. "They're saying 'Who?'"

But that didn't bother John. After all, he had achieved his dream of making it to the NBA. The long nights spent shooting baskets in the driveway on North Superior Street had finally paid off. To succeed in the pros, however, he would need to add an extra dimension of toughness to his game. What was more, as a playmaker, he would have to find a special teammate to whom he could distribute the basketball. Preferably someone big, with the powerful moves to get to the hoop and score. That person would turn out to be someone very different from John Stockton. He came from a very different part of the country, with a very different background, but with the same passionate love of basketball. His name was Karl Malone.

3

Just country People

Like John Stockton,

Karl Malone had a basketball hoop hanging in the backyard of his childhood home. But his was just the twin ends of an old bicycle spoke, twisted into a hoop, hanging from a tree. He built the hoop after his mother got tired of standing around with her arms making a circle so Karl could shoot ball after ball. But Karl's life was a lot different from John Stockton's.

Karl Malone was born on July 24, 1963. He grew up in the small town of Summerfield, Louisiana, near the Arkansas border. Karl was the seventh of nine children. He had four brothers and four sisters.

When Karl was four years old, his father, J.P. Malone, abandoned the family. As a result, Karl's mother, Shirley Malone, had to raise all nine children by herself. Shirley believed in teaching her children by example. Her fundamental lessons were what she called "bedrock religion and the value of hard work." During the day, she worked in a nearby sawmill. At night, she had a job cutting up chickens. She even took a third job running machinery, just to be able to provide for her large family without assistance from the government.

"A social worker came once and said, 'Did you know you qualify for welfare?'" Shirley Malone later recalled. "I said it was *my* responsibility to take care of my children. I believe every tub should sit on its own bottom."

Because of this sacrifice and hard work, Karl feels he owes his mother an enormous debt of gratitude. "I saw my mother wear cardboard in her shoes, just so each of us could have a good pair," he said. "I saw what the water did to that cardboard. I can never repay her."

The Malones lived in a big white house in the Louisiana woods. They grew a lot of their own food in a large garden alongside the house. There were collard greens (Karl's favorite), corn, potatoes, and many other vegetables. The Malones also had a chicken coop and a pen full of hogs. Collecting the eggs from the henhouse and feeding the chickens were two of young Karl's many household chores.

Growing up, Karl Malone was like most other active country boys. He liked to roam around outside with his friends, catching frogs and lizards. There were all kinds of squirrels, raccoons, and other animals in Summerfield to keep a young boy occupied. At the age of five, Karl eagerly learned to fish and hunt.

Along with a love of the outdoors, Karl also developed a nose for mischief. Once, Karl, his brother Terry, and another friend sneaked into a neighbor's watermelon patch when the man wasn't home. They smashed open one watermelon, ate it, and then started busting up all the watermelons in the patch. When the neighbor found out, he told Karl's mother. But he refused to take money from a family that had so little. So after giving each of her sons a sound whipping, Shirley Malone made them lug firewood to the man's house every day for six months as a way of repaying him.

As he got older, Karl found different kinds of trouble to get himself into. Shooting out windows with BB guns and chasing cows were just some of the pranks he tried. Through it all, Shirley Malone's punishments were strict. "From when I was twelve till I was seventeen, if we went a day and a half without getting a whupping, something was wrong with us," Karl remembered. Fortunately, Karl never got into any trouble with the law. He never did drugs or drank, for instance.

Helping keep the family on an even keel was Shirley's new husband, Ed Turner, whom she married when Karl was 12. Ed was a plumber, but he aspired to run his own business. Together, Shirley and Ed opened up Turner's Grocery & Washeteria. Ed hoped that Shirley would ease up on her grueling work schedule. But she insisted on working more than 60 hours a week in the shop. Again, Karl took note of her example.

Karl would get his chance to apply the value of hard work when he entered Summerfield High School. Hoping to make the school basketball team, Karl found his path blocked by his poor grades. Too many nights spent getting into trouble rather than doing his homework had left him without the "C" average required to participate in after-school athletics. Karl was disappointed, but refused to apply himself to his studies.

The boy's basketball coach, Howard Moss, could see that Karl had the potential to be a great player. So he intervened on Karl's behalf, encouraging him to hit the books, instead of just coming to Summerfield games to watch the other boys play. By the middle of his sophomore year, Karl was finally getting Coach Moss's message. He raised his average grade up above a "C" for the first time and was declared eligible to play sports.

In Karl's first season with the Summerfield Rebels, he averaged more than 15 points a game. His scoring presence proved to be just the edge the Rebels needed to advance into the state basketball playoffs. Though the team was only one game above .500 for the season, they roared into the Louisiana state Class C championship game and a matchup with their archrivals, Pineview High. In a tightly played contest, Karl's rebounding prowess provided the difference in Summerfield's 63–62 overtime victory.

Karl's junior year was even better. With the help of Coach Moss he improved his low-post offense, learning to cut down on his lateral movement and take the ball straight up to the basket. He became a better rebounder as well. The only flaw in Karl's game was his tendency to get into foul trouble. This kept him on the bench for crucial stretches in many Summerfield High games. Nevertheless, the Rebels won their second-straight state title, defeating Pineview again, 70–67, in the championship game.

In his senior year, Karl capped off a trifecta of **High school tRifecTa** state titles by leading Summerfield to a 60–46 blowout win over Fenton High. For the season, he averaged 32.4 points and 18.0 rebounds a game. The word "dominant" does not begin to describe his level of play. In one game, he torched an opponent to the tune of 49 points; in another, he plucked a school record 37 rebounds off the backboard. College scouts began to pay close attention to the muscular teen who by now was 6 feet 7 (200 centimeters) tall.

That left Karl with a decision. Where should he go to school? He narrowed his choices to two schools, Arkansas and Louisiana Tech. Arkansas was an NCAA basketball powerhouse, the kind of program that can pave a player's path to the NBA. Louisiana Tech was, well, it was close to home. In fact, its women's basketball team was better known than the men's squad. But the campus was only 40 miles (64 kilometers) away in nearby Ruston, close enough that Karl could easily get to Summerfield.

After Karl had initially committed to go to Arkansas, his mother convinced him to change his decision. She didn't want Karl to travel that far from home. Karl would later admit that she was right.

"I wanted to stay near home because, deep down, I'm a small-town guy who wants to be near friends and relatives," he said. "The bright lights of the big city are really not for me. I like it when you can walk down a street and say hello to everybody."

Karl enrolled at Louisiana Tech in the fall of 1981. He lived on campus, took out a bank loan to pay for his tuition, and seemed set to live the life of a highly coveted basketball prospect. There was just one catch. His high school grade-point average was

.03 point under the minimum required of varsity athletes. Reluctantly, the Tech basketball staff informed him he would have to sit out a year and maintain good grades in order to join the squad the following fall. It was like freshman year of high school all over again. Except this time, Karl saw the hardship as a challenge, not a source of frustration.

"That was the best thing that ever happened to me," Karl said of not being able to play. "My last years of high school, I was starting to think I was better than other people, that I was special and things would just come to me." Another time, he observed, "I went around thinking, 'Hey, I'm Karl Malone and I don't have to do school work.'"

Even though he couldn't play, Karl worked hard. He was able to improve his grades, majoring in elementary education. And he spent much of his time in the weight room, developing his powerful upper body. By the start of his sophomore year in college, he was raring to take the court. The yearlong layoff, he later said, "made me a hungry player."

In 1982–1983, Karl dominated his college opponents just as he had in Louisiana high school competition. Playing center, he scored 20.9 points a game while hauling down 10.3 rebounds. More important, Tech had a record of 19–9, good enough for second place in the Southland Conference. In an unprecedented honor, the conference named him both Newcomer of the Year and Most Valuable Player.

In his second season of eligibility, Karl continued to improve. Again he averaged the magic "double double"—double figures in both points and rebounds—that marks the superior frontcourt player. And Tech, feeding off the double teams that now swarmed on him whenever he touched the ball, began playing better as a team.

KARL BEGAN SHOWING HIS STRENGTH AND REBOUNDING SKILLS AT LOUISIANA TECH. ONCE IN THE NBA, HE BECAME AN OUTSTANDING REBOUNDER WITH A REAL NOSE FOR THE BASKETBALL.

The Bulldogs went 26–7, won the Southland Conference championship, and secured the first NCAA Tournament bid in the school's history. While they lost in the second round to the mighty Houston Cougars of Hakeem Olajuwon and Clyde Drexler, they had established themselves as a force to be reckoned with on a national level.

The 1984–1985 season turned out to be Karl's last at Louisiana  Tech. It was also the year he earned the nickname "the Mailman." A sportswriter who had to struggle through inclement weather to watch him clean the backboards and dominate the low post decided that, no matter what the conditions were outside, Karl would "always deliver." The name stuck, and continues to be true to this day.

What Karl "delivered" in his final year with Tech was 16.3 points a game, 9.3 rebounds, and a litter of shattered backboards from his mighty dunks. NCAA fever reached the point that Tech began mailing out shards of broken glass to the team's supporters to keep as souvenirs. Not surprisingly, Louisiana Tech again followed their big man's lead. For the third year in a row, the team's record improved, this time to 29–3. They were ranked in the top twenty and had earned another trip to the annual NCAA National Championship Tournament.

"March Madness" gripped Louisiana hard, as the Bulldogs bested perennial powerhouses Pittsburgh and Ohio State to move into the "Sweet 16." It was an amazing accomplishment for a small school with a previously insignificant basketball reputation. And even though Tech lost to Oklahoma by two points to end their season, fans around the country had had a chance to see them play.

NBA scouts were able to see them play as well. And the player they were most interested in was Karl Malone. That left Karl with another decision to make. Because he had been barred from playing during his first year at college, he had the option of returning to Louisiana Tech for a fourth year of basketball eligibility. With his grade-point average up near a 3.0, he certainly would have no trouble staying on the team. But Karl decided to test the waters of the 1985 NBA draft. He was convinced he could make it in the pros.

When draft day arrived, Karl was sure he would be one of the first ten players chosen. But as the draft progressed, he watched as less talented prospects like Joe Kleine, Jon Koncak, and Kenny Green were selected ahead of him. Karl began to worry that he would *never* be chosen. "I got scared, sitting there thinking, 'Am I going to be a big fluke?'"

Some NBA officials were puzzled as well. Frank Layden, the coach of the Utah Jazz, was watching the draft that day. "As I watched guys go ahead of Karl, my first reaction was, why? Is there something the matter with this guy? Is there something about this guy we don't know? Is he sick or something?" Like John Stockton the year before, Karl seemed to have suffered for having gone to a small school without a major basketball reputation. Nevertheless, Layden and the Jazz were happy to be in position to take him. Picking thirteenth, they made Karl their first selection. Other teams would later offer a variety of explanations for passing on Karl Malone. In most cases, they came to regret their decision.

Though he would have liked to have been a Top Ten pick, Karl was happy to be part of an NBA team at last. He knew little about the Jazz, except that they had moved from his home state of Louisiana in 1979. "I'm looking forward to playing in the town of Utah," he told Layden after he was selected, showing how little he knew about the state he was about to call home.

Just like John Stockton, Karl Malone was a draft day surprise that had fallen into Utah's lap. On these two mid-first-round picks, taken a year apart, they were to stake all their hopes for the future. Each man had to endure his own NBA growing pains, however, before their partnership could really begin.

4

A two-man Jazz band

John Stockton arrived in his first NBA training camp with something to prove. To himself if no one else.

"The only person in the *world* who thought John would play in the NBA was John," his father once said. Nevertheless, here he was, already penciled in as the team's backup point guard for the 1984–1985 season.

That year, veteran Rickey Green ran the Jazz's dynamic fast-break style offense. Forward Adrian Dantley, a master of the post-up game, was the club's primary scoring option, with jump-shooting guard

Darrel Griffith providing instant offense from the outside. In this system, the point guard's job of bringing the ball upcourt to find the open man for quick scoring chances became crucial. At 6 feet 1, John knew that he would face a physical challenge from bigger and stronger NBA players. One way he could compensate for that was to rely on hard work and intelligence.

Two days after the draft, he had asked the Jazz to send him a set of game films. By the time he arrived in camp three months later, he had studied all the team's plays. He knew where Dantley and Griffith liked to get the ball. And he had impressed the Jazz coaching staff with his preparation and knowledge of the game.

To help ease his adjustment to the pros (and to ward off any hint of controversy) John quickly made friends with Rickey Green. In fact, they had lockers next to each other at the home arena, The Salt Palace (named after Salt Lake City, the capital of Utah) from John's earliest days with the team. John would learn a lot from Green, who was coming off an All-Star season in which he had led the Jazz to the Western Conference semifinals.

Coming off the bench in all 82 games, John enjoyed a fine rookie season. He averaged 5.6 points and 5.1 assists in 18.2 minutes of action. He established Jazz rookie records for total steals

JOHN WAS ALWAYS
A GREAT PLAYMAKER
BUT ONCE HE

and assists, with 109 and 415, respectively. While the Jazz struggled to a fourth-place tie for the regular season, they upset the heavily favored Houston Rockets in the first round of the playoffs. They were once again eliminated in the semi's. In ten playoff contests, John averaged 6.8 points and 4.3 assists in relief of Green.

The next year, John faced an even tougher test. He knew he had to raise the level of his game and establish a foothold in the NBA for years to come. But he was up to the challenge. He improved his scoring and assist averages to 7.7 and 7.4, respectively, as his minutes on the court rose to 23.6, or more than half the game. In effect, he was splitting point guard duties with Rickey Green, and the team was showing no ill effect. In fact the Jazz improved their record by one win in the regular season, but were bounced by the Dallas Mavericks in the first round of the playoffs.

The main bright spot for the Jazz in 1985–1986, however, was the emergence of another rookie, forward Karl Malone. Unlike John, Karl knew there weren't many physical obstacles to his succeeding in the NBA. At 6 feet 9, he was big enough to match up against the league's other power forwards. No, his growing pains were mainly matters of psychological adjustment to his new surroundings.

"I was nervous when I first came to Utah," he later admitted. An African-American from rural Louisiana could easily be unnerved in a state that was 92 percent white. "In fact, it took me a week-and-a-half to see the first black person. And he was a bag man on the street. I was so happy to see a black face that I spoke to him for two hours."

But Karl was soon won over by the friendliness and family atmosphere of his new home town. "The best thing that could have happened to Karl Malone," he would later say, "was coming to Salt Lake City."

Like John, Karl came to camp expecting to play a backup role for the team, who already had Adrian Dantley to do most of the low-post scoring. But Karl's strong play in the Jazz's opening two games, including an 8 point, 6 rebound effort against the Houston Rockets, forced coach Frank Layden to insert him into the starting lineup, opposite Dantley.

Karl was tested early and often by the league's other power forwards. One of them, Maurice Lucas, had a reputation as an enforcer, a player who guards the low post with the ferocity of a lion guarding its den. In one early season contest, Karl was scoring on Lucas at will. Finally, after having yet another rebound ripped away from him by the upstart rookie, Lucas had had enough. "Stop going over me," he snarled, "before I hurt you." But Karl would have none of his threats. He immediately steamed down the court and dunked in Lucas's face. It was a statement to the rest of the league. Karl Malone would not be intimidated.

By December, the Mailman was really delivering. In fact, he played so well that he was named NBA Rookie of the Month. There were still rough edges in his game. "He'd knock away rebounds from his own people, miss breakaway dunks," said Layden, "and his foul shooting was awful. But I have been around basketball long enough to know that all Karl needed was growing up."

Helping Karl to grow up on the court was easygoing Adrian Dantley. Just as Rickey Green had shown John the ropes, Dantley tutored Karl in how to play certain opponents, when referees were apt to call certain fouls, and how to adjust to the fast pace and heavy travel of life in the NBA.

As a rookie, Karl did not always take winning and losing as seriously as he should have. "I wanted to be an athlete just to make money," he later admitted. But when the Jazz traded Dantley in the off-season, making Karl the focus of their offense, "all of a sudden not just a little responsibility was on me, but now a great deal. It's a situation where I asked myself, 'What do you really want in life? Do you want to just please Karl Malone, or do you want to touch other lives?'"

KARL WAS A DOMINANT PLAYER RIGHT FROM HIS ROOKIE YEAR OF 1985–1986. HE MADE THE ALL-ROOKIE TEAM, AND WHEN HE WENT HARD TO THE HOOP, PEOPLE GOT OUT OF THE WAY.

All in all, it had been a successful rookie season for Karl. He averaged 14.9 points and 8.9 rebounds per game and made the NBA All-Rookie team. He finished third in Rookie of the Year voting, and contributed a game-winning turnaround jumper in the Jazz's lone playoff victory against the Mavericks, a shot he called "my biggest thrill ever." He was rewarded with a new $275,000 contract for 1986–1987.

That season was one of transition for both Stockton and Malone. John inherited the starting point guard spot from Rickey Green. But he still had to split time with the veteran, a setup that gave the Jazz one of the most intimidating point-guard tandems in the league. Green was the more reliable scorer, averaging 9.6 points in 25.8 minutes of action. John was the more accomplished playmaker, setting up his teammates with 8.2 assists in 22.7 minutes a contest, while tacking on 7.9 points. For the season, he averaged only 5.6 shot attempts a game.

But with Karl establishing himself as an offensive force, the Jazz did not need their point guard to score. Helped along by John's crisp, pinpoint passes, the Mailman upped his own scoring average to 21.7 points a game. Another of the factors motivating him was coach Layden's demand that he become the team leader. Once the Jazz pilot even threatened to trade Karl if he didn't work harder to improve his game. "That threat became Malone's challenge," wrote one local sportswriter.

Karl went on a weightlifting and training binge, designed to add more power to his already sculpted body. He began to study the game more, learning how to avoid cheap fouls in order to stay on the floor during "crunch time." Most importantly, he earned the respect of opponents around the league with his work ethic and diverse range of skills.

"Karl does so many darned things for a big guy," observed Los Angeles Lakers general manager Jerry West, after a 1986 Jazz-Lakers game. "He runs the court, passes the ball, shoots it well. He's improved tremendously over last year."

Not that Karl and John didn't find time for a little fun, as well. For John, fun could mean fixing up his house. Like the time a friend drove by and saw him hanging off the roof, applying siding.

"Bet the Jazz would love that," John thought.

As for Karl, the off-season was the time to "partay"—although his version of "hard living" often meant spending time with his family. One of his favorite haunts was Monopoly's Park Place, a nightclub near his home in Dallas. Fashionably late, he would pull up in his deep-red Mercedes-Benz 560 SEL and meet, not some movie actress or rock star, but his sister and brother. Neither member of this classic NBA tandem could exactly be called a social ball of fire.

The Jazz finished the season with a 44–38 record, good enough for second in the NBA's Midwest Division. They drew the Golden State Warriors in the first round of the playoffs. Their series would provide a taste of the kind of one-two punch that Stockton and Malone were to provide in the years to come. John shot a sizzling .621 from the floor for the series. He averaged 10.0 points and 8.0 assists for the five games, prototypical point-guard numbers. The recipient of many of those assists was Karl. In Game One, he threw a "20 and 10" on the hapless Warriors, who were blown out at the Salt Palace, 99–85. Lumbering 7 foot 4 (218 centimeters) center Mark Eaton and veteran Rickey Green also came up big for Utah.

When the Jazz took Game Two as well, it looked like they were on their way to the next round. But it was not to be. Despite huge efforts by Stockton and Malone, Utah fell prey to hot shooting by Golden State in three straight heartbreaking losses. They even had to suffer through a Game Five loss on their home court. John and Karl found the second consecutive early exit from the playoffs hard to accept. Each man vowed that the next year would be different.

The 1987–1988 season *was* different. The Jazz had their best season ever, and John and Karl emerged as the most feared guard-forward tandem in the NBA. The team's spirited postseason run saw them take the defending world champion Los Angeles Lakers to a seventh game in the conference semifinals.

How did they improve so much so quickly? Off the court, both players worked hard to improve their games. John, for example, spent his summer working out in the Gonzaga gym. Some people began writing that he had reached his limits as a player, but he was determined to prove them wrong.

 A breakthrough year by John Stockton was also largely responsible. In 1987–1988, he finally wrested full-time control of the Jazz offense from the aging Rickey Green. Perhaps more important, because of their close friendship, the changing of the guards was accomplished without any jealousy or rancor.

"It's obvious that the tide has turned here and John has emerged," Green commented during that season. "The change is so justifiable, there's nothing anybody can say." At this point, it was clear that the Jazz could no longer afford to have John Stockton be a bench player.

With increased playing time (up to 34.7 minutes per game from 22.7 in 1986–1987), John saw his shooting stroke improve dramatically. Always a superb passer, he had now become a jump-shooting threat with three-point range. During one 24-game stretch in midseason, he hit an incredible 66 percent of his shots and never shot less than 50 percent in a game. He finished the year averaging a career-high 14.7 points per game.

"It's not so much how well John is shooting it as when he's shooting it. He's really making good decisions," said Rickey Green of John's new offensive mind-set.

His ability to make shots improved John's playmaking as well. As defenders learned they could not leave him unguarded on the outside, passing lanes opened up for him to dish the ball off to open teammates.

The result was an astonishing total of 1,128 assists for the season, shattering the NBA record of 1,123 held by Detroit's Isiah Thomas. Laker Magic Johnson, the NBA's other prestige point guard of the 1980s, saw John blow by him for the assists-per-game lead with 13.8. Steals were another part of John's arsenal, as he averaged nearly three thefts per game, good enough for third in the league.

John's performance was surprising to some, but not to those who knew him best. "Every year he's just gotten better," said his old Gonzaga coach, Dan Fitzgerald. "It's like he's on a ladder, going one step at a time."

"It wasn't all just feeding a post-up player," beamed coach Frank Layden of John's assist totals. "It's been scattering the ball. The way we run our break, it could be confusing, because sometimes we have two and three men on one side of the floor. He seems to dish it off to the right guy."

"John can let guys cross and go through and, all of a sudden, bang, something happens for him," gushed Jazz assistant coach Jerry Sloan. "From that standpoint, I'd say he's probably the best I've ever seen." Layden, Sloan, and the rest of the Jazz hierarchy were looking more and more like masterminds for picking the slick Spokane product in the draft four years earlier.

Who was the principal beneficiary of Stockton's improved play? Why, Karl Malone, of course! The hungry Mailman needed to be fed constantly, and his favorite snack was a juicy pass served up by chef John Stockton. Karl threw down a career-high 27.7 points a game, as fans around the league increasingly came to see him and Stockton as a potent one-two combination. And while it's true that Karl benefited enormously from having John in the backcourt, he had more than enough skills to adapt to any environment, as he showed in his first All-Star Game appearance in Chicago. Without John's assistance, he still managed to record 22 points and 10 rebounds. The great thing about the Stockton-and-Malone partnership was the ability of two men with enormous individual talents to mesh so perfectly together for the good of the team.

Truth be told, it took a while for that to happen. For while their stars were playing at a high level, the Jazz limped into the All-Star break with a 22–22 record. They turned it around in the second half of the season, however, riding eight straight 30-point games by Malone at the close to finish up at 47–35. It was their best record as a franchise, good enough for third place in the Midwest Division, and it gave them a wave of momentum going into their opening round playoff series against the Portland Trail Blazers.

The Blazers proved no easy match, going down in four spirited contests, as Karl dominated the post. But the team's semifinal series against the Lakers was to prove a real surprise. The Jazz extended the defending champs to the full seven games, largely on the play of their "one-two punch."

Karl was a monster in game two, which the Jazz won, 101–97, on the Lakers's home floor in Inglewood, California. His 29 points in that game represented his average for the series, in which he also hauled down 12 rebounds per contest.

Game five belonged to Stockton. He dished out an incredible 24 assists, tying the playoff record

BY 1988, JOHN HAD
BECOME ONE OF THE
BEST PASSERS IN
THE LEAGUE. IN A
PLAYOFF GAME

held by the man who was guarding him, Magic Johnson. Amazingly, the Jazz lost that game, 111–109, as the clock ran out while John scrambled around looking to make the tying field goal. Still, Stockton averaged 19.5 points and 14.9 assists for the series.

After rallying to tie the series in game six, led by Karl's 27 points (and his inspirational promise of victory), Utah went down to defeat in game seven. Again, Karl was great, pouring in 31 points and grabbing 15 rebounds. But it was the Lakers that went on to win their second-straight NBA championship.

Though they headed home to Utah short of their own championship goal, the Jazz had a lot to be proud of. Karl Malone summed up their 1988 spirit in an interview several years later. "We played together as a team, and we believed in each other on and off the court. However, the Lakers had a far better team."

The Lakers may have had more talent. But with John and Karl leading the way, the Jazz were beginning to learn that teamwork has its rewards. In the coming years, they would spread that lesson around the rest of the NBA.

AGAINST THE LAKERS, HE TIED A RECORD WITH AN INCREDIBLE 24 ASSISTS.

bEauTiful MuSic

By the time of their 1989 All-Star coming-out party, John and Karl had earned the respect of the rest of the NBA. Widely regarded as the best guard-forward tandem in the game, they were also beginning their tenure as the league's longest-running mutual admiration society.

"I've never seen Karl tired," John remarked of his partner's physical condition. "He's on a different standard than the rest of us."

Of the Mailman's ferocious style of play, John observed, "I've never seen Karl physically dominated in a game. Yet he's not walking around trying to bully people. Karl has risen above all of us."

Karl was equally complimentary of his buddy Stock.

"What John Stockton doesn't know," Malone confessed in an interview, "is that he is like one of my older brothers to me, and not because he gives me the ball on the break. Mess with Stockton and you mess with me."

On the court, basketball's answer to Lennon and McCartney had showcased their unique relationship in a November 1988 game against the Phoenix Suns. Karl notched a career-high 42 points in the 134–121 victory, while John dished out 21 assists. "We could never stop them," marveled coach Cotton Fitzsimmons of the Suns. "Malone was a monster and Stockton was a monster." The "monster mash" that followed in February at the All-Star Game merely let the rest of the country in on the secret.

Another way in which John and Karl were tied was their strong commitment to family. In 1986, John married Nada Stepovich, his college sweetheart. They bought a house on North Superior Street in Spokane right next door to his parents' place. Every summer after the basketball season, the couple returned to Washington, where John spent most of his time working on the house or drilling basketball fundamentals into the players at Gonzaga. Down at Jack & Dan's Tavern, posters of John began adorning the walls at his first blush of NBA success. A satellite dish piped in all Utah Jazz telecasts.

Karl used the fruits of his first big NBA contract to take care of his family back in Summerville. He bought his sister Jenny a red sports car to take her back and forth to beauty school. And he purchased a house in Dallas where he could stay in the off-season, just a three-hour drive from the family home. His mother would make the drive to Karl's house on Sundays to prepare a good country dinner for Karl and his brothers and sisters.

When it came time to marry, after several years as Utah's most eligible bachelor, Karl finally tied the knot with model Kay Kinsey, the former "Miss Idaho." During the season, the couple shared a home in Salt Lake City with a family of a different sort: Karl's pets Jazzmine the Rottweiler, Maggie the Eel, Pete the Lobster, and Nikki the Python. Not to mentioned several unnamed piranhas.

In Chicago at All-Star Weekend, Karl showed the world his admiration for his parents by inviting his mother and stepfather up on stage with him for the postgame press conference and his acceptance of the Most Valuable Player award. "I brought my mother to sit up here for a reason," he announced as he accepted the MVP trophy. "When

I was growing up, she worked two jobs and still found time for me. A lot of people would pass by and say, 'What is she doing? He's never going to amount to anything.' Well, I guess they were wrong. I may be from the country, but for one day I'm king of the city."

That season, piloted by a new coach, former Chicago Bulls guard Jerry Sloan, the Jazz were kings of the Midwest Division. They finished at 51–31 on the strength of quintessential Stockton and Malone performances. John led the NBA in assists, with 13.6 per game, and steals, with 3.2 per contest. Meanwhile, Karl upped his scoring average to a lofty 29.1 points, second only to Michael Jordan. Nevertheless, the Jazz were swept in the first round of the playoffs by the surprising Golden State Warriors.

Unfortunately, 1989–1990 was to be a bad rerun of that disappointment. Again, the Jazz had a fine regular season, winning 55 games and losing only 27. Again, their dynamic duo put up stellar numbers. John averaged an NBA record of 14.5 assists a game, becoming the first man ever to notch 1,000 total assists for the third time. (He built on his own record by doing it the next two seasons as well.) Karl saw his scoring average improve to 31 points per game, as he became the first man since Elgin Baylor in 1963 to average over 30 points and 10 rebounds for a season. But once again, the Jazz were ousted in the first round of the playoffs, this time by a determined Phoenix Suns team led by brash point guard Kevin Johnson.

Adding insult to injury, Karl was not voted to the Western Conference All-Star team. While John was chosen by fans to start for the first time ever in the contest, Karl found himself outpolled by A.C. Green of the Lakers for the honor. His pride was stung by the snub. "This is a slap in the face," he declared, and immediately went out and dropped 61 points on the hapless Milwaukee Bucks. A minor injury kept him out of the All-Star festivities entirely.

The Jazz played the entire 1990–1991 season in the shadow of that playoff failure. The team acquired sweet-shooting guard Jeff Malone (no relation to Karl) in the off-season to take some of the load off John and Karl. At first, the new player had trouble blending in as Utah struggled, losing 7 of its first 15 games. But the team blossomed in the winter months, going on a 21–9 tear through January and February. For the season, Karl averaged 29 points and 11 rebounds, while John upped his scoring average to 17.2 with an NBA record 1,164 assists. Jeff Malone contributed mightily, with 18.6 points of his own per contest. The Jazz cruised to a 54–28 record and shook a major monkey off their backs by dispatching the Suns in the opening round of the playoffs.

BY THE EARLY 1990s, KARL HAD BECOME A FORCE, BUTTING HEADS WITH THE LEAGUE'S BEST POWER FORWARDS. HERE HE SCORES AGAINST CHARLES BARKLEY, WHO WAS THEN A MEMBER OF THE HOUSTON ROCKETS.

The semifinals provided an all-too-familiar lesson in frustration, however. A determined Portland Trail Blazer squad secured its place in the conference finals with a convincing five-game series victory. It was losses like this that caused some around the NBA to question the heart of Jazz.

"Utah has been known to crumble at the end," crowed one player, San Antonio Spurs Terry Cummings. And Chuck Person of the Indiana Pacers claimed the Jazz would never win an NBA title because Karl Malone would "back down" under pressure. Karl was quick to respond to the team's critics.

"I'll sum it up by saying that I have more class than Chuck Person," he thundered. "Every year, we have a winning team, and that's important. Can Chuck Person say that? No!"

John was more philosophical in responding to the team's inability to get that elusive championship ring.

"I'd like to win one, but if that's the only way you can put a positive value on yourself, then you're in big trouble."

The two shining stars of the Utah Jazz lineup may have had difficulty propelling their team to the finals, but they had no difficulty collecting individual honors. In October 1991, they received one of the greatest of them all, as both John and Karl were selected to the U.S. men's Olympic Basketball Team.

The "Dream Team" as it would be known, was

the first Olympic squad to include professional players. Magic Johnson, Larry Bird, and Michael Jordan were just some of the big-name teammates who would join Stockton and Malone in the 1992 Games at Barcelona. For Karl, it was sweet retribution because he had been cut from the team after trying out for the 1984 Olympic squad.

John's selection caused quite a bit more controversy. The thirteen-member selection committee had bypassed another premier point guard, Detroit's Isiah Thomas, in favor of the Jazz playmaker. Some pundits saw the hand of Magic Johnson, Isiah's bitter rival, in the snub, but few could dispute John's qualifications for the honor. Typically, he refused to get embroiled in the dispute. "I haven't been involved in any controversy," he told the *Sporting News*. "It had nothing to do with me. The thing with Isiah was between him and the committee. I wasn't involved."

Isiah Thomas was to be a key figure in Karl Malone's 1991–1992 season as well. In a mid-December game in Utah, the all-star Piston drove toward the basket for what looked like an easy layup. Then Karl stepped in. He collided with Isiah in midair, fouling him hard with his right elbow. The resulting gash above Isiah's right eye required 40 stitches to close. Karl was assessed a flagrant foul, fined $10,000, and suspended by the league for one game. After the game, he insisted he had not intended to hurt Isiah.

"It was an accident. Right after, I called Isiah and everything was settled. He said, 'Karl, I know what kind of player you are. Don't worry what people say.'"

Nevertheless, the incident confirmed the belief of many around the NBA that Karl was a dirty player. It was a charge that was leveled at John Stockton as well. Many players were irritated by John's ability to blow past them off the dribble, or by his aggressive, jersey-grabbing, lead-with-your-elbow style.

"Stockton's as mean as they come," Dennis Rodman once said. "Everybody might think he's a choirboy, but he'll slip you an elbow when the refs aren't looking, or he'll talk some junk. I like that in a guy."

"Stockton's one of the dirtiest players in the league," claimed another NBA point guard.

"That's ridiculous," was John's reply to such charges. "I hope I'm an irritating player. But dirty? Not even close."

The physical play of Utah's "bruise brothers", as *Sports Illustrated* dubbed them, led the Jazz to another fine season in 1991–1992. Playing in a new arena, the 19,000-seat Delta Center, Utah received valuable contributions from new players Tyrone Corbin and David Benoit. Club president Frank Layden called that year's edition "the best team we have ever had." They defied their critics by taking the Midwest Division crown with a 55–27 record. Karl poured in 28 points a night, while John led the league in steals and assists. Both players made the All-Star team.

When the playoffs rolled around, the Jazz were smoking. They were on a 26–10 tear going into the annual postseason tournament. Karl sensed a different atmosphere than in years past. "I have a better feeling now than the year we took the Lakers to seven games."

He was right. The Jazz fought off the pesky Los Angeles Clippers in the first round, then steamrolled the up-and-coming Seattle SuperSonics in the Western Conference semifinals. Now they would play the Portland Trail Blazers for the right to advance to the championship series.

It was the first time in the conference finals for John and Karl, and to no one's surprise they came up big. The Jazz fought back from a two-game deficit, winning the next two games. But in game five, John got poked in the eye during the second quarter and was unable to continue playing. Deprived of his ability to dish and drive—he averaged 14.8

points and 13.6 assists for the postseason—Utah fell in overtime, 127–121. They lost Game Six on their home floor and with it the series.

Not even an Olympic triumph could ease the sting of another playoff loss. The Dream Team romped easily to a gold medal. Karl led the team in rebounding in three of the lopsided contests. And John, though he played sparingly due to a newly healed broken leg suffered in the qualifying round, was right there on the stand to accept the gold medal symbolizing international athletic achievement.

Somehow it seemed fitting that John and Karl should take their unparalleled two-man game to the international stage. They had already shown the NBA and the rest of America the benefits of their hard-nosed, team-oriented brand of basketball. Now the world could see them as well. All that was left, besides the elusive title, was to secure their places in basketball history.

6

SETTING
the Standard

In 1992-1993, the Jazz were struggling through a disappointing season. They would finish the year in third place, at 47–35, and be eliminated by Seattle in the opening round of the playoffs. But like clockwork, their two leaders were putting up their usual impressive statistics. When All-Star Weekend rolled around in February, all of Utah basked in the national spotlight. The game took place at the brand-new Delta Center in Salt Lake City, and the more than 19,000 fans in attendance wanted America to know how much they appreciated their state's two most famous goodwill ambassadors.

"I get nervous before every ballgame," said the Mailman. "But before this one I had more butter-flies than normal. I don't know if it was the fans' cheering or what. But I was more nervous than I was even before my first NBA game."

Of the thunderous ovation that greeted their introduction, John Stockton said, "I tried not to think about it. If I started thinking about being nervous, my brain would have just clouded over."

When the game began, Western Conference coach Paul Westphal called John's and Karl's num-bers—again and again.

"You have to give a lot of credit to coach Westphal," Karl said. "I don't know how many times he ran that 34 play [the basic play in the Jazz of-fense], but he ran it to death."

But for the funky All-Star uniforms, it looked like a typical Utah Jazz home game. Karl poured in a team-high 28 points, snatched 10 rebounds, and blocked 2 shots. John contributed 15 assists, 6 re-bounds, and 2 steals. When the game went into overtime, he took over. He scored a pair of clutch baskets and assisted on two others as the West pre-vailed, 135–132. After the game, a panel of 11 jour-nalists named John and Karl co-MVPs.

To win a joint MVP on their home floor, in front of a national audience, made it especially meaning-

KARL, WITH DAUGHTER KAYDEE, HELPS JOHN

HOLD THE 1993 NBA
ALL-STAR GAME TROPHY.

ful. To do it against the elite players of the NBA gave it added drama. And to do it together made it typical Stockton and Malone.

"I can't speak for Karl, but being able to win it with him makes it more special for me," John observed.

"You can't have the chicken without the egg," Karl added. "You can't have one without the other."

When it came time for one of them to carry home the MVP trophy, Karl let John do the honors. "I've got one already," he said. "I can go home and rub mine if I want some of that feeling. I'll let Stock have this one."

The next morning, David Moore of the *Dallas Morning News* summed it up best. "Malone and teammate John Stockton went out Sunday afternoon and made sure their fellow All-Stars knew who rules in Salt Lake City."

The Jazz climbed back to the top of the Western Conference in 1993–1994. They improved their record to 53–29 and battled their way into the conference finals. There they were eliminated by the Houston Rockets, four games to one. John led the NBA in assists, with 12.6 per game, while Karl poured in his customary 25.2 points, grabbing 11.5 rebounds per contest.

Then, in 1994–1995, there was a season of milestones for both Jazz superstars. On January 20, 1995, in a home game against the Cleveland

Cavaliers, Karl became the 19th player to record 20,000 career points. The final point came on a free throw, and set off a frenzy of celebration in the packed Delta Center. Karl's teammates took time out to honor his achievement.

"It's a nice bump in the road," said a nonplussed Mailman afterward. "I'll stop for a second and look at the bump, but I won't get out of the car."

Less than two weeks later, John had his turn to celebrate. On February 1, he became the NBA's all-time assist leader, notching his 9,922nd career assist in a home game against the Denver Nuggets. The lucky recipient? Karl, of course, who scored from the left corner just as he had on so many other picture-perfect Stockton passes through their ten years of playing together.

John had entered the game 11 assists behind the career leader, Magic Johnson. But he obliterated the record before halftime, with a little help from teammates anxious to put the milestone behind them.

"My teammates were going to make sure the record happened," John said after the game. "It wasn't me. There were some wonderful shots tonight, some I won't soon forget."

Magic Johnson himself delivered a taped message congratulating John on his achievement. An electric Delta Center crowd went wild at the sight of their old playoff nemesis on the scoreboard screen.

Around the country, sportswriters devoted columns to singing John's praises. They began to rank him among the all-time great point guards, like Johnson and Oscar Robertson, "the Big O." John shook off the comparisons with typical humility.

"I don't think of myself near those other point guards," he observed. "Once you start thinking you're good, that's when you get hammered."

Others were not so modest. "We had a saying in high school and college," Karl told an interviewer, "'make your teammate an All-American,' and in this case, 'make your teammate an All-Star,' and Stock is one of those guys. He always tries to go out and make his teammates All-Stars. People ask me what I would be without him, and I don't even want to think about it."

Karl, meanwhile, was quietly going about his business. He produced his usual awesome numbers in 1994–1995—26.7 points and 10.6 rebounds per game—despite a swirl of trade rumors at the start of the season. Rumors of bad blood between the Mailman and Jazz owner Larry Miller stopped circulating as the power forward led the team to a franchise record 60 wins, two games behind San Antonio in the Midwest Division. Yet another early playoff exit—this time to the defending champion Houston Rockets—turned a successful campaign into a frustrating one.

The 1995–1996 season saw John Stockton add another record to his growing collection. On February 20, 1996, he broke Maurice Cheeks' mark with his 2,311th career steal. He was now the NBA's all-time leader in both assists and steals. The record-breaker came in a home game against the Boston Celtics, when John slapped the ball out of the hands of Eric Williams along the baseline. The theft led to a Jazz three-pointer at the other end. It was typical Stockton—fundamentally executed and perfectly timed.

Utah produced a 55–27 season, once again finishing second to San Antonio in the Midwest Division. John won his ninth straight league assist crown, while Karl was an all-NBA first team selection for the eighth consecutive year. There was no doubt that each player had cemented his place in league history. Their only piece of unfinished business was bringing an NBA championship to an otherwise successful franchise.

The always-vocal Jazz fans had, in fact, adopted a new slogan during the year. NOW IS THE TIME banners were seen all over the Delta Center. Some felt that with John at 34 and Karl at 32, time was running out. But Karl said otherwise.

"Maybe I'd be worried about that if I thought this was our last chance," the Mailman said. "But John and I have some years left. We're going to try

THOUGH NEVER A FLASHY PLAYER, JOHN COULD MAKE SOME SPECTACULAR SHOTS.

our best to get it this year, just as we always do, but if we don't get it, we'll be back taking another run next season."

Utah opened the 1995–1996 playoffs with a best-of-five series against the Portland Trail Blazers. The opening game was typical of the Jazz and their two veteran stars. Utah won it, 110–102, as Stockton scored just 11 points but had an amazing 23 assists. Malone led all scorers with 33 points on 14 for 21 shooting, and added 9 rebounds.

But the series wasn't a walkover. Portland fought back and it finally came down to a fifth and decisive game at the Delta Center. With a capacity crowd of more than 19,000 screaming fans behind them, the Jazz romped, winning by a 102–64 count. Karl had 25 points and 10 rebounds, while John added 21 points, 11 assists and a pair of steals. The old reliable one-two punch had led Utah into the next round. But that one wouldn't be easy. The Jazz now had to meet division champ San Antonio, led by 7-foot-1 (216 centimeter) superstar center David Robinson, in a best-of-seven series.

The Jazz surprised a lot of people when they went into the Alamodome and took away San Antonio's home-court advantage by winning game one, 95–75. As usual, they were led by Stockton and Malone. John had 13 points and 19 assists, completely outplaying the Spurs point guard Avery Johnson. Karl had 23 points, but did a stellar job defending against the taller Robinson.

"I just try to frustrate him a little," Karl said, "make him work for everything he gets."

Though the Spurs bounced back to win the next game, Utah took the next pair at the Delta Center for a 3–1 lead. San Antonio managed to win one at home, but back at the Delta Center for game six, the Jazz ended it. They won easily, 108–81, taking the series and making it to the Western Conference finals for the third time in five years.

Now the Jazz had to go up against the powerful Seattle SuperSonics for the Western Conference crown. Seattle had a 64–18 regular-season record, second only to the incredible 72–10 mark achieved by the Chicago Bulls in the Eastern Conference. Not only were the Sonics favored over the Jazz, but they, too, were led by a combination point guard and power forward. In the eyes of many, Gary Payton and Shawn Kemp were the heirs apparent to Stockton and Malone. And, at age 27 and 26, they were considerably younger.

The four players were all great, but performed with a different style. As veteran Sonics forward Sam Perkins said:

"Stockton and Malone set the standard for how a point guard and power forward should play together, and Gary and Shawn are what that combination has evolved into. Stockton and Malone are more conservative, and Gary and Shawn like to do their thing with a little more flair, which is the way the NBA has gone these days. You can't say one way is better than the other; they're just different."

That was true. John and Karl played basic, old-fashioned basketball. They used tried-and-true plays such as the pick-and-roll. Payton and Kemp preferred the fast break and alley-oop pass, often resulting in a thunderous slam-dunk.

Karl admitted that Kemp had become a superior player and when reminded that many still considered the Mailman the best in the game, Karl said, with a wink, "Yeah, but I'm old."

John, also, frowned on comparisons. In fact, he rarely said much when it came to analyzing his game.

"I don't care what people say about me, and I don't care about individual matchups," he told a reporter. "I just play."

Yet the younger Payton showed the kind of respect everyone in the league had for John. Known for "trash talking" on the court, taunting his opponents, Payton stayed uncharacteristically quiet when he played against John. When asked why, he said, simply, "He's the best. I'm still looking for a real weakness in his game. If there's one guy I want to be like, it's Stockton."

But coming into the series with Seattle, John was not 100 percent. He was nursing a sore hamstring and bruised elbow, among other things, and it would affect his play. But like his teammate Malone, he wouldn't complain, wouldn't make excuses, and wouldn't think of coming out of the game.

The first two games of the series didn't go well at all for the Jazz. Playing before a hostile crowd at Seattle's Key Arena, the Jazz were blown out of game one, 102–72. It was their worst loss of the entire season. While Karl played Kemp to a virtual standoff, each scoring 21 points, John began showing the effects of his nagging injuries. He had just 4 points on 2-of-10 shooting and garnered only 7 assists. Payton, on the other hand, had 21 points.

Game two was closer. Seattle hung on for a 91–87 victory as Karl scored 32. But John again disappointed. After scoring 9 points in the first quarter he all but disappeared. He added only two more the rest of the way and committed seven turnovers. Again, there were no excuses, but those who knew John best saw that he was bothered by physical problems. He just couldn't go all out.

Returning to the Delta Center for game three, the Jazz looked like a different team. They came out of the gate quickly and cruised to a 96–76 victory, cutting the Sonics lead to 2–1. Karl had 28 points and 18 rebounds, while shooting guard Jeff Hornacek also broke out with 28 points.

But game four proved to be a real heartbreaker. Despite the raucous Utah fans, Seattle held an 8-point lead going into the final quarter. Then the Jazz battled back. With 12.2 seconds left, Seattle had an 88–86 lead, but the Jazz had the ball. A two-point field goal would tie the game, a three-pointer would win it. But John missed a long, 25-footer at the buzzer and the Sonics now had a 3–1 lead in the series.

"The shot was straight, no question about it, just a little short," John said, afterward. "That's not what we were looking for, but it was certainly makable."

No excuses, as usual. John, however, had just 7 points in the game. He was not playing well. Worse yet, the Jazz were one game from elimination. Yet they didn't quit. They returned to Seattle and upset the Sonics in overtime, 98–95, as Karl had 29 points and 15 rebounds. Hornacek again came up big with 27 points, while John had just 4 points and 6 assists. One newspaper headline went as far as to say: *Hornacek Making Up For Sorry Stockton.*

Once again, John made no excuses for his play. He simply praised his teammate. "We certainly know how good [Hornacek] is," John said. "We'd have been in deep trouble without him."

Back at the Delta Center for game six, John had his best outing of the series. Not surprisingly, the Jazz won easily, 118–83, to tie the Sonics at three games each. Stockton had 14 points and 12 assists to go with Malone's 32 and Hornacek's 23. Now it came down to just a single game for the right to go to the Finals.

"It's just like any other game," John said. "I always try to simplify and make it a one-game series, and that's what we're down to."

"The odds were against us," Karl added. "Nobody expected us to win up there, but we did. It shows a lot of character about this team."

The final game was played at the Key Arena with the Sonics again favored. Despite being on the road, the Jazz played with fire and confidence. The game was close all the way. With 8.2 seconds left, the Sonics had an 89–86 lead. Then Karl was hacked going to the hoop. Two free throws would have brought the Jazz within one, but he missed both. A final Seattle free throw made it 90–86 when the buzzer sounded. The Jazz had fought their hearts out, but came up short.

When it was over, Karl still held his head high. "We won like men, we lose like men," he said. "We played hard but didn't get it done."

It was another big disappointment for the Jazz and their two superstars. True, the team had lost again. But in 18 playoff games Karl averaged 26.5 points, second only to Michael Jordan, and also grabbed 10.3 rebounds a game. And John, despite his injuries, still had 10.8 assists per game, tied with Kevin Johnson for the best in the playoffs.

There were those who said that John's age was beginning to show, that Payton had exposed him as a player whose skills were slowly eroding. Utah coach Jerry Sloan was quick to come to his point guard's defense.

"They said [Payton] was doing a great job defending him," Sloan said, "but [John] couldn't straighten his arm out for six weeks, his shooting arm. Let him straighten his arm out and see how he would have played."

So the two veteran stars licked their wounds during the off-season. When they returned for 1996–1997, each was determined to show there was still a lot of basketball life inside him. Once again, there was something to prove, another challenge over the horizon. Both John and Karl wouldn't want it any other way.

7

a place in history

Prior to the 1996-1997

season, the so-called experts didn't expect anything different from the Jazz. In fact, a number of pre-season polls indicated the Jazz would take a step backward, primarily because the team's two superstars were getting older. A *Sports Illustrated* preseason look was typical. The Jazz were projected to finish third (behind San Antonio and Houston) in the Midwest Division. The preview said, in part:

"The Jazz has a solid supporting cast, led by guard Jeff Hornacek, but it will go only as far as its aging stars, power forward Karl Malone and point guard John

Stockton, can take it. Stockton . . . appeared tired in the postseason (in 1996). Malone . . . was inconsistent in the Western Conference finals."

But perhaps those who were making predictions didn't really know about the competitive fires that still burned in the hearts of both players. Neither was motivated by money any longer. With escalating NBA contracts, both had all they would ever need. John's contract called for him to earn $6 million in the upcoming season. Karl's called for nearly $5 million, the difference simply a matter of when their last pact was drawn. Both were among the top wage earners in the league.

Now the motivation was simply their pride and a desire to see a championship banner raised to the rafters of the Delta Center. Away from the action, both led very stable lives, almost conservative by the standards set by many other high-priced athletes. Both were devoted to family, though some of their interests were quite diverse.

John was the consummate family man. He and his wife now had four children—sons Houston, Michael, and David, and daughter Lindsay. After games, John would usually change into a polo shirt and jeans and leave the arena in a plain Chevy Suburban. No fancy jewelry or flashy cars for Stockton. As one writer put it, "He is an ordinary man, the antithesis of the stereotypical star athlete."

"He likes being home with us," his wife, Nada, has said. "He also loves playing basketball and other games with his children, but never pushes them to try to equal his achievements."

"I don't crush the kids," John says of their playtimes. "But I do want them to know that they have to earn what they get. I tell them I'm happy if they just do the best they can. My parents were that way with me."

John does have, however, one rather adventurous hobby. He enjoys flying, to the point where in the summer of 1996 he took command of an F-16 fighter jet. He had help and guidance from a pilot in the Air Force's elite Thunderbird unit. John admired the pilots for the ease in which they did their jobs.

"They're normal guys outside the plane," he said. "But inside they're pretty special. When you watch them, you realize it takes only the slightest touch to do some amazing things. It's like everything else, I guess. When you get guys who are the best in the world at what they do, they make it look easy."

Which is the way John plays basketball. His still-boyish looks often hide the intense competitor inside him. Always in tremendous physical condition, John is the Jazz champion on the treadmill. He holds the team record and enjoys defending his title every year. His conditioning and determination are the reasons he has missed just a handful of games during his long career.

Karl, too, is a devoted family man. Though his tastes are somewhat like the man himself—big—he spends time with family and relatives when away from the court. Karl has a fleet of Harley-Davidson motorcycles and often drives one to and from home games. He'll wear jeans, a leather jacket with fringes, and silver-toed cowboy boots. And he loves riding one of his Harleys on the open road, especially after losses.

OFF-COURT, JOHN SPENDS A LOT OF TIME FLYING, WHILE KARL LIKES TO PILOT ONE OF HIS FLEET OF HARLEY-DAVIDSONS.

"Sometimes when things get a little tough, I just do that," Karl has said. "It's just good being outdoors."

Love of the countryside and outdoors has led Karl to keep a ranch in his home state of Louisiana and a log cabin in Alaska. He is currently building a beautiful, 16,000-square-foot (1,486-square-meter) "dream house" in Utah. It will be made of logs, river rocks, and oak. When someone marveled at the size of the house, Karl, without intending to brag, said simply, "I've earned it."

The big guy also has his own 18-wheel tractor-trailer, custom-painted with psychedelic images and fully outfitted inside, even down to a fax machine. The 64-foot (20-meter) rig always attracts a lot of attention on Utah's highways.

"Yeah, it gets some stares," Karl says, "but I wanted something special."

The price has been more than a decade of banging heads with the biggest, strongest power forwards and centers the NBA has to offer. Not an easy task. But like John, Karl keeps in tiptop condition with an off-season regimen that includes 400 sit-ups a day. He also runs ten 100-meter dashes; three 200-meter dashes; and three 300-meter dashes as part of his workout. In the weight room he curls 60-pound (27 kilogram) dumbbells, and presses some 270 pounds (120 kilograms). He does this over and over.

"I like doing it," Karl admits. "I see myself improving. I feel the power and strength growing."

And like his much smaller teammate, Karl very rarely misses a game. Both players believe that the fans pay good money to see them on the court, not on the bench or in street clothes nursing minor injuries. As John proved in the 1995–1996 playoffs, he'll go out there hurting, even if he isn't 100 percent. The Mailman has done the same thing.

So coming into the new season both players felt they were ready to give it another shot. Neither was about to make any concessions to age. And they had some solid support. Jeff Hornacek was back at shooting guard. Byron Russell at small forward seemed ready to become a star. Second-year center, Greg Ostertag, at 7 feet 2 (218 centimeters) was a much-improved player and a big body in the middle. Veterans Antoine Carr, Chris Morris, and Greg Foster, along with youngsters Howard Eisley and Shandon Anderson, gave the team depth. As far as the players and Coach Jerry Sloan were concerned, this was a team ready to make a serious run at the title.

At the outset of the season Utah's great twosome received yet another honor. They were among the players selected as the NBA's 50 best of All Time. In addition, longtime basketball writer Pete Vecsey also included the duo on his list of the 50 greatest ever. So there was no little doubt about their ultimate place in the game. Someday, the two will be enshrined in the Basketball Hall of Fame in Springfield, Massachusetts.

But that is still years away. It became apparent as soon as the season started that both John and Karl were once again in top form, and the rest of the Jazz followed their lead. Utah jumped atop the Midwest Division and was playing as well as any team in the NBA this side of the Chicago Bulls. Karl was second in the league in scoring behind Michael Jordan, while John was battling for the assist lead with Denver's Mark Jackson. Suddenly, it was as if people were rediscovering these amazing teammates all over again.

In picking his Fab Fifty list, Pete Vecsey described Malone this way: "Flaunts more dimensions than the prototype power forwards who preceded him. Capable of beating up opponents inside, beating them outside or beating them down the floor."

Of Stockton, Vecsey wrote: "Only point guard to set picks on power forwards, enabling Karl Malone to shake free. Despite rough stuff, he's only missed four games in 12 seasons. . . .Uncommon determination and an exceptional comprehension of the game."

The one play that Stockton and Malone ran better than perhaps any duo in the history of the game was the pick-and-roll. With the pick-and-roll, a player sets a pick, or screen, for the dribbler and then rolls to an open spot, looking for a return pass and an easy basket. To set a pick, a player simply plants himself on a spot and the dribbler moves past, causing his defender to either run into the man setting the pick (a foul), try to fight his way through, or go behind the man setting the pick.

This can enable the dribbler to get free for a jumpshot or drive to the hoop. Sometimes the defender guarding the man setting the pick will switch and pick up the dribbler. If the set-up man is big like Karl, he may suddenly have a much smaller man guarding him. And if the ball handler is swift, like John, he may find himself with a bigger, slower defender that he can easily beat.

Karl and John have worked this play to perfection over the years. Karl usually sets the pick, then rolls off to receive one of John's crisp passes. It's impossible to count the number of dunks, easy layups, or short jumpers that Karl has made via the pick-and-roll. As former Celtics great Bob Cousy said, "Malone comes out and sets that big pick, and Stockton handles the ball like a world-class violinist."

As the season continued it became more apparent that John and Karl were having outstanding years. Only the Jordan-led Bulls had a better record than the Jazz. Karl was so good, in fact, that many began saying he should be the league's Most Valuable Player, an award all but conceded to Jordan after the season began.

During the final months of the regular season it was Karl who was getting the most ink. Yet the Mailman was always quick to praise his longtime teammate who was always getting him the ball. "[Stock's] as steady as the ticktock of a clock," was the way Karl put it. "Other [point guards] come into the league, and they've got the flashy moves and the endorse-

KARL HAS MADE MANY SHORT JUMP SHOTS LIKE THIS ONE AFTER WORKING THE PICK-AND-ROLL WITH JOHN. THE TWO RUN THIS BASIC PLAY AS WELL AS ANY DUO IN NBA HISTORY.

ments. Then they come play against John, and he teaches them that you can play this game without putting the ball between your legs 20 times before you do something with it. He just keeps making the plays, game after game, year after year."

The Jazz kept up their outstanding play all year. Once again both John and Karl played all 82 games and the team won the Midwest Division with a 64–18 mark, their best ever. They also had the best record in the Western Conference and would have the home court advantage right through the Conference Finals. Only the Eastern Conference Bulls at 69–13 had a better record.

It had certainly been a banner year for Karl Malone. The Mailman averaged 27.4 points a game, second to Jordan's 29.6. He was sixth in field goal percentage (55.0) and eleventh in rebounding with 9.9 caroms per game. But that didn't tell the whole story. After a dozen years in the league, Karl was starting to write a story of greatness.

His 2,249 points in 1996–1997 was the tenth-straight season he had topped the 2,000 point mark. That was an NBA record. In addition, he moved past the legendary Jerry West and into 10th place on the all-time scoring list. Better yet, he also became one of just five NBA players to have more than 25,000 points and 10,000 rebounds for his career. The others in that exclusive club were Wilt Chamberlain, Kareem Abdul-Jabbar, Moses Malone, and Elvin Hayes, all Hall of Famers. And, of course, the Mailman was a first team All-NBA selection once again.

John didn't have the same kind of individual numbers as Karl, but had another fine season nevertheless. He averaged 10.5 assists a game, but for the first time in a decade wasn't the NBA leader. He was edged by Mark Jackson, who played for both Denver and Indiana during the season. John was also seventh in field goal percentage (54.8) and eighth in steals with 2.2 per game. Karl continued getting much of the ink. It reached a climax shortly after the playoffs began, when the Mailman was named the league's Most Valuable Player, edging Michael Jordan in a close vote.

KARL ACCEPTS THE MVP TROPHY, SHARING THE MON WITH HIS MOTHER, SHIRLE (LEFT), AND HIS WIFE, KAY.

At the age of 33, Karl was the oldest player ever to receive the coveted award, and John Stockton was the first to give his teammate full credit.

"Obviously, with the MVP, [Karl] has gotten a lot of attention. But he's deserved it. . . . He's carried this team for a long time, and we all play off of him as a team. . . . [The MVP award] is due."

Karl was touched deeply by winning the MVP. Still, he was able to joke when he said, "I thank Michael [Jordan] for letting me borrow this for one year," then adding, "To have this trophy after 12 years, really and truly I never thought I'd have the opportunity."

The individual honors done, it was time for unfinished business—trying to win a championship. It started well as the Jazz eliminated the Los Angeles Clippers in three straight games. Now, however, they had to go up against the Los Angeles Lakers, led by their superstar center, Shaquille O'Neal. Many felt that the Lakers had the firepower to pull off an upset.

But this version of the Jazz was different. Whatever caused some of the past Utah teams to take an early exit from the playoffs was gone. More experience, better support players, a deeper bench—these factors helped to give the team balance. But, in the end, it was still the Stockton and Malone show. The team would go as far as the two stars could carry it.

The tone was set in game one. Utah handled the Lakers easily, winning by a 93–77 count. Karl had 23 points and 13 rebounds to lead the way. But more impressive was the fact that 8 different players scored eight or more points for the Jazz. The hoop that finally put it out of reach came with 2:26 left in the final quarter. John stole a Lakers pass and fired a sharp pass to Karl for a thunderous dunk that made the score 86–72. After the game, John spoke about his team's quest for the championship.

"Maybe some things are different this year," he said. "But are a deep bench and intensity keys to a championship team? I don't know. I haven't been on one yet. I hope I'll be able to answer that question for you before too long."

It was apparent the Jazz wanted to make quick work of the Lakers. They won a close second game, 103–101, then faltered in the third. Back in Los Angeles, the Lakers won easily, 104–84, as Karl hit just 2 of 20 shots from the floor and John missed all six shots he took. That made game four all important, and the Jazz came up big.

They outscored the Lakers in all four quarters, winning handily, 110–95. Karl led the way with 42 big points, including a playoff record 18 straight from the foul line. Byron Russell supported him with 29, while John had 11 assists. That was all the Jazz needed. They won the next two games to eliminate the Lakers in five, 4–1. The finale was a 98–95 overtime victory in which Karl had 32 points and 20 rebounds, while John chipped in with 24 points and 10 assists. The longtime teammates had done it again.

Now it was on to the Western Conference Finals. That was where the Jazz always hit the wall. They had lost the conference finals three times in the last five years. This time they would be meeting a veteran Houston Rockets team. The Rockets were led by three aging superstars of their own—center Hakeem Olajuwon, forward Charles Barkley, and guard Clyde Drexler. Houston had won a pair of NBA titles in 1994 and 1995, so they knew what it took. It would be a tough nut for the Jazz to crack.

The series opened at the Delta Center, and the Jazz made the first one look easy. They took command in the second quarter and cruised to a 101–86 victory. Karl had a relatively quiet game with 21 points and 13 rebounds, but his teammates picked up the slack. Hornacek had 19, and John had 16 points and 13 assists. In fact, he completely outplayed Houston's rookie point guard Matt Maloney and ran the offense with swift precision.

Then in game two, John really began to assert himself. He scored 26 points, had 12 assists and 8 rebounds as the Jazz won again, 104–92. Suddenly, it was as if he turned back the clock. He was playing with sheer brilliance, and the Jazz had a 2–0 lead in the series.

Back at the Summit Arena in Houston, the Rockets rallied to win both the third and fourth games. The third one was easy, 118–110, but the fourth was a battle, with Houston's Eddie Johnson winning it with a long three-pointer at the buzzer, 95–92. But no one could deny the continued brilliant play of John Stockton.

At one point in game four, John ran the pick-and-roll on four straight possessions. Each time he pulled up and nailed a jumper. He scored 22 that night and was averaging 21 points for the series.

Back in Utah for game five, the Jazz took a close one, 96–91, with John again the star. He hit 6 of 7 shots from the field, his final hoop a beautiful drive between Barkley and Maloney that helped put the game on ice.

"I try to exploit things against everybody, that's part of the game," he said. "Beat the guy that guards me while you're beating their team."

Now the headlines were markedly different. A year earlier, when John was injured, a newspaper called him "Sorry Stockton." After game five, a headline read: *Stockton Carrying Jazz In West Finals*. He did it again in game six. Playing back in Houston, Utah upset the Rockets, 103–100, to take the series. This time John hit the game-winning shot, a 25-foot three-pointer just as the clock wound down. Even better, 15 of John's team high 25 points came in the final quarter when his team needed him the most. Karl played his usual strong game with 24, but this time the hero of the game was Stockton.

"John Stockton is one of the five best players I ever played against," said Charles Barkley, himself a future Hall of Famer.

But it didn't really matter who the hero was. The Jazz were in the NBA Finals at last with a chance to win that elusive title. Waiting for them, however, was basketball's best team and its greatest player. The defending champion Chicago Bulls, led by Michael Jordan, were favorites to win their fifth NBA championship of the 1990s.

The entire state of Utah now had Jazzmania. Vicki Varela,  a spokesperson for Governor Mike Leavitt said: "We decided to declare a 'Utah Jazz Year' regardless of the outcome [of the Finals]."

Some 15,000 fans were waiting at the airport at 5:15 A.M. when the team returned from their victory over Houston.

"Unbelievable," Karl said, looking at the crowd. "At 5 o'clock in the morning to have this many people here is just unbelievable."

IN GAME ONE OF THE FINALS, STOCKTON AND

But in game one, the Jazz would have to deal with the hostile crowd at the United Center in Chicago. Still, they played the Bulls extremely tough. The game was tied at 82 when Karl was fouled with just 9.2 seconds left. To the dismay of the Jazz fans and players, both shots rolled off the rim. Seconds later, Jordan hit a clutch jumper at the buzzer to give the Bulls an 84–82 victory.

Despite scoring 23 points and grabbing 15 rebounds, while outplaying Chicago's Dennis Rodman, Karl was disappointed. But, as always, he didn't make excuses.

"It was agonizing," he said, "but I won't dwell on it. They were big free throws. . . I just didn't make them. It's behind me now. . . I just want to find consistency. . . I've been through a lot of adversity. It's going to take a lot to break this nut. I want to have the opportunity to go to the line again."

Once again John had been outstanding, with 16 points and 12 assists, including a clutch three-pointer that gave the Jazz the lead at 82–81. But a loss is still a loss. It became worse when the Bulls won the second game, 97–85, with Jordan scoring 38. But the next three games would be played at the Delta Center. Winning all three at home was Utah's only chance.

MALONE PLAYED BRILLIANTLY TOGETHER, BUT LUCK WASN'T ON THEIR SIDE THAT NIGHT.

Sure enough, the Jazz won the

third game, 104–93, with Karl scoring 37 big points. Then came game four. It was a low-scoring, rugged defensive battle. With little time left, the Bulls had a 71–66 lead and appeared ready to pull away. That's when John took over. He hit another big three-pointer, bringing it back to 71–69.

A short time later, with the score 73–69, he stole the ball from Jordan and went the length of the court. Jordan fouled him as he went up for the shot and he made one of two free throws, making the score 73–70. Then, 28 seconds later, John was fouled again. This time he made them both, and the Jazz trailed by just a single point. Next, John made the play of the game.

He grabbed the rebound on a Jordan miss and looked upcourt. Karl was streaking ahead of everyone with Jordan in pursuit. Without pause, John fired a long pass downcourt. It had to be perfect. Karl caught it in mid-stride and went in for a layup to give the Jazz the lead at 74–73. Then, with 18 seconds left, Karl got the chance to redeem himself as he made two clutch free throws to put it on ice. The final was 78–73. Utah had tied the series. After the game, everyone was talking about John's magnificent pass.

"Would I have made that pass?" Jazz forward Byron Russell asked. Then he answered his own question. "I'm not John Stockton."

Stockton admitted that if anyone other than Karl had broken free he wouldn't have thrown the ball.

"I saw Karl had position, and when he does, he's the best at getting the ball. I had great faith that he would fight for the ball and come down with it."

As for Malone, he had nothing but praise for his teammate. "I knew Michael was lurking," the Mailman said. "But I also knew that if anybody could get that pass to me, it was Stock. When he threw it, I thought, 'Well, Stock doesn't throw bad passes, so I must be open.'"

Unfortunately, the game would be a last hurrah. When a flu-ridden Jordan scored 38 points in game five, it inspired his teammates and led to a 90–88 Chicago victory at the Delta Center. It was Jordan's three-pointer with 25 seconds left that iced the game in one of basketball's most remarkable performances. Back in Chicago for the sixth game, the Bulls won it, but not without a battle.

This time Jordan scored 39 as the Bulls took another close one, 90–86, to repeat as champions. But the Jazz had done themselves proud. They lost the final two games by a total of six points. That's how close they were to winning the title. And while Jordan and Scottie Pippen might still rank as the top one-two punch in the league, Stockton and Malone were not far behind. Both had played their hearts out and could feel proud of what they had done.

The achievements of John Stockton and Karl Malone are already legendary. Seldom have a pair of all-star performers worked together so well for so long. There has never been an angry word between them, and fingers have never been pointed.

"We don't talk a lot on the court," Karl has said. "We talk a lot away from the game. When things are bothering us, we tell each other. We just say it and go out to play, and play to win. Not one time did we look back and say, 'It's your fault.'"

As John has said, "I'm going to compete. I'm fortunate to be on a team where everybody comes to compete. Where do we get that? Probably from our parents, from our families and some friends we knocked heads with from the first grade.

"I don't think age is a hindrance. Maybe physically we can't do things exactly the way we could 10 years ago, but there are other things you gain with experience. You learn to be a better player when you don't have the same raw physical skills."

And Karl spoke for both of them when he said, "We don't want to leave this game owing anything. We want to be able to say that we gave the game of basketball everything we had, and in return the game gave us everything. We're even. Because that's how we came into this league and that's how I want to go out. I can speak for Stock because I know him well enough to know he'll say the same thing."

Both John and Karl gave their all again in 1996–1997, when they took the Jazz to within a few points of an NBA title. They have not only meant so much to each other and the game of basketball, but these unique teammates have also meant a great deal to the state of Utah.

Perhaps it was former NBA player and current Jazz broadcaster "Hot Rod" Hundley who said it best. Talking about what John and Karl have meant to the community and to Salt Lake City, Hundley quipped: "Someday, people in this town are going to be meeting at the corner of Stockton and Malone."

As a tribute, that would be entirely fitting.

inDex